THE SYNOD OF ROME (610 AD)

St. Boniface IV,

Bishop of Rome

Translated by: D.P. Curtin

Dalcassian
Publishing
Company

PHILADELPHIA, PA

ISBN: **978-1-960069-81-8** (Paperback)

Library of Congress Control Number:
Author: Curtin, D.P. (1985-)

Printed by Ingram Content Group, 1 Ingram Blvd, La Vergne, Tennessee

First printing edition 2019.

Introduction

Little is known about the Synod of Rome in 610 AD, beyond a few terse references. Unlike the more famous Synod under Pope Damasus, it did not have far reaching consequences for the Latin church, or even for the diocese of Rome. However, it is clear that some minor assembly of bishops met with the Pope. What survives here in these documents does not appear to be the legitimate records of that gathering. No canons are granted, nor are there any points of theological doctrine discussed. Instead, the primary cause of this synod is noted tersely, and then the discussion switches to the authority of the king to protect the immunity of the church. Without delving into the original manuscripts too deeply, these works do seem suspect, and they sound like Anglo-Catholic reactions to the dissolvement of the monasteries under Henry VIII, and are therefore ecclesiastical products of the 16th century, and not of the early 7th century. Certainly, the absence of references to these documents prior to the Tudor period would speak to their spurious origin.

D.P. Curtin
October 31, 2019
Wexford, PA

The case of the Church of England celebrated in Rome, in the 8th year of Phocatus as emperor, by the 13th indictment, and on the third day of the month of March, promoting the English cause, and among us in the same sitting Mellitus the first bishop of London.

The canons or the decree of this council are not found, but after finishing what he writes about Lawrence, the archbishop of Canterbury, Bede proceeds thus, book II, chapter 4:

At this time Mellitus, bishop of London, came to Rome to negotiate with the apostolic pope Boniface about the necessary causes of the English Church. The same most reverend pope compelled a synod of the bishops of Italy to create order for the life of the monks and their quiet. Mellitus himself sat down among them in the eighth year of the reign of prince Phocatus. By indictment on the thirteenth day of March, on the third day of the month of March, that all the decrees were duly confirmed by his own authority. Returning to Britain, he would bring with him the orders and observances of the English Church, together with the letters which the same pope had addressed to God's beloved archbishop Lawrence, and to the whole clergy. Likewise this was sent to King Edilbert and the nation of England. This is Boniface, the fourth from the blessed Gregory, bishop of the city of Rome, et cetera.

DECREE OF THE SYNOD,
promulgated in the Roman Council III.
In the month of March in the year of Christ 610

How is it permissible for monks to serve everywhere with the priestly office?

There are some who claim, supported by no dogma, indeed, very boldly, inflamed with zeal more of bitterness than of love, who assert that monks, because they are dead to the world, and live to God, are unworthy of the power of the priestly office. By this, neither penance, nor Christianity can be bestowed, nor can they absolve themselves by the power divinely enjoined by the priestly office. For if for this reason the old rivals had preached the truth, the most blessed Gregory of the apostolic see, powerful in monastic worship, would by no means have ascended to the highest peak. For indeed he had the power to act, to bind, and to loose these things is granted by God in the highest degree. As Augustine [of Canterbury] also, a disciple of the most holy Gregory, an excellent preacher of the English, and the most blessed Martinus of Pannonia, whose reputation for sanctity spread far and wide throughout the world personifies. Others as well, already shining in the most holy and most precious habit of monks, would by no means be bound by the priestly ring, because they were monks, they were forbidden to use the aforesaid. Benedict, the preceptor of the monks, did not in any way forbid such a thing. He declared that they would only be experienced in worldly affairs. This, indeed, by the apostolic documents, and by the institutions of all the holy Fathers, is very much enjoined, not only on the monks, but also on the canons. For no one who serves God involves himself in worldly affairs. And both of them, even by the clear examples of the aforesaid Fathers, it is predicated on all sides that they are dead to the world with the most evident reason. Therefore, by the examples set by so many of the Fathers, which it is dangerous to contradict, we believe that the duty of binding and releasing monks by the priests is not unworthily administered by the commanding will of God, if it happens that they are dignified for this service. This is affirmed by anyone who clearly considers the state of the monks and the behavior of the powerful. For example: an angel in Greek, a messenger in Latin. Therefore the priests, monks and canons, who daily proclaim the holy precepts of God, are called angels, for a reason that is not incongruous. The closer each angelic order is contemplated to the glory of God, the more exalted it is affirmed in dignity. In order to use the cherubim, the monks are covered with six wings. Two, indeed, in the chapter in which the head is covered, are demonstrated by probable assertions. That part of the tunic which is extended by the arms, we say to be two wings, and that last part by which the body is placed is said to fill the number of six wings with certainty. Therefore, contending that the priests of the monastic profession should be kept from the duty of priestly power, we order them in every way to restrain them from such nefarious ventures in the future, because the higher each one, the more powerful he is.

LETTER FROM THE SAME COUNCIL GIVEN TO ATHELBERT, KING OF ENGLAND.

To the most excellent and excellent king of the English, Athelbert Bonifacius, bishop, servant of the servants of God:

While the integrity of your Christianity has so grown around the worship of its founder, that it shines far and wide, and is announced in all the world, reporting the stages of your activity worthy of God. We give enormous thanks to God, the giver of all good things, who looked down on you from on high and raised you to such a height of virtue. Therefore, glorious son, we willingly grant what you requested from the apostolic see through our co-bishop Mellitus. That is, that your kindness in the monastery established in the city of Doroverne (Canterbury), which your holy teacher Augustine, a disciple of Gregory of blessed memory, consecrated to the name of the holy Savior, of which our most beloved brother Lawrence is acknowledged to be presiding at the present time, may lawfully by all means establish a habitation for monks living regularly. It is decided, by apostolic authority, that they themselves should be preachers of your salvation. They will associate a flock of monks to themselves, and they will clothe their holy life as well as their morals. If any one of the successors of your kings, whether bishops, clerics, or laymen, has attempted to nullify all these decrees, let him be subject to the bond of anathema by Peter, the chief of the apostles. This Peter, and by all his successors, until he repents of what he has done with a rash venture, with satisfaction pleasing to God, and makes true amends for this disquiet. May you be strong in Christ, my dear son.

LATIN TEXT

CONCILIUM ROMANUM SUB BONIFACIO IV.

In causa Anglicanae Ecclesiae celebratum Romae, anno 8 Phocatis imperatoris, indictione 13, et tertia die Kalendarum Martiarum, rem Anglicam promovente, et in eodem consedente Mellito primo episcopo Londinensi.

(Non reperiuntur istius concilii canones vel decretum, sed finitis quae scribit de Laurentio archiepiscopo Cantuariae, Beda sic progreditur, lib. II, cap. 4.)

His temporibus venit Mellitus Londoniae episcopus Romam, de necessariis Ecclesiae Anglorum causis cum apostolico papa Bonifacio tractaturus. Et cum idem papa reverendissimus cogeret synodum episcoporum Italiae, de vita monachorum et quiete ordinaturus, et ipse Mellitus inter eos assedit anno octavo imperii Phocatis principis; indictione decima tertia, tertia die Kalendarum Martiarum, ut quaeque erant regulariter decreta sua quoque auctoritate subscribens confirmaret, ac in Britanniam rediens, secum Anglorum Ecclesiae mandata atque observanda deferret, una cum epistolis quas idem pontifex Deo dilecto archiepiscopo Laurentio, et clero universo, similiter et Edilberto regi atque genti Anglorum direxit. Hic est Bonifacius quartus a beato Gregorio Romanae urbis episcopo, etc.

DECRETUM SYNODI, Promulgatum in concilio Romano III. Kal. Martias anno Christi 610.

Quomodo liceat monachis cum sacerdotali officio ubiubi ministrare.

Sunt nonnulli fulti nullo dogmate, audacissime quidem, zelo magis amaritudinis quam dilectione inflammati, asserentes monachos, quia mundo mortui sunt, et Deo vivunt, sacerdotalis officii potentia indignos, neque poenitentiam, neque Christianitatem largiri, neque absolvere posse per sacerdotali officio divinitus injunctam potestatem: sed omnino labuntur. Nam si ex hac causa veteres aemuli vera praedicarent, apostolicae compar sedis beatissimus Gregorius monachico cultu pollens ad summam nullatenus apicem conscenderet. Quoniam quidem haec ostiatim fungendi, ligandi, solvendique potestas a Deo summa conceditur. Augustinus quoque ejusdem sanctissimi Gregorii discipulus, Anglorum praedicator egregius, ac Pannoniensis Martinus beatissimus, cujus sanctitatis fama longe lateque diffusa totus personat mundus; alii quoque jam plurimi sanctissimi pretiosissimo monachorum habitu fulgentes nequaquam annulo pontificali subartarentur, si quia monachi fuerunt praedictis uti prohiberentur. Neque enim Benedictus monachorum praeceptor almificus hujuscemodi rei aliquo modo fuit interdictor; sed eos saecularium negotiorum edixit expertes fore solummodo. Quod quidem apostolicis documentis, et omnium sanctorum Patrum institutis, non solum monachis, verum etiam canonicis maximopere imperatur. Nemo enim militans Deo implicat se negotiis saecularibus. Utrisque etiam praefatorum Patrum exemplis perspicacibus circumquaque ut mundo mortui sint evidentissima ratione praecipitur. Tantorum igitur Patrum instituti exemplis, quibus periculosissimum est refragari, credimus a sacerdotibus monachis ligandi solvendique officium Deo imperante haud indigne administrari, si eos digne contigerit ad hoc ministerium sublimari. Quod incunctanter affirmat quisquis statum monachorum et habitum potentatum que evidenter considerat. Verbi gratia: angelus Graece, Latine nuntius dicitur. Sacerdotes igitur monachi atque canonici, qui quotidie sancta Dei praecepta annuntiant, angeli vocantur, ratione non incongrua. Sed unusquisque angelicus ordo quanto claritatem Dei vicinius contemplatur, tanto dignitate sublimior affirmatur. Nam uti cherubim, monachi sex alis velantur. Duae quidem in capitio quo caput tegitur verisimilibus demonstratur assertionibus. Illud vero tunicae quod brachiis extenditur, alas duas esse dicimus: et illud tandem quo conditur corpus, sex alarum numerum certissime implere asseritur. Decertantes igitur monachicae professionis presbyteros sacerdotalis potentiae arcere officio, omnimodo praecipimus, ut ab hujuscemodi nefandis ausibus reprimantur in posterum, quia quanto quisque celsior, tanto potentior.

EPISTOLA EX EODEM CONCILIO DATA AD ATHELBERTUM, REGEM ANGLORUM.

Domino excellentissimo atque praecellentissimo regi Anglorum Athelberto Bonifacius episcopus servus servorum Dei.

Dum Christianitatis vestrae integritas ita circa conditoris sui cultum excreverit, ut longe lateque resplendeat, et in omni mundo annuntiata, vestrae Deo dignae operationis augmenta referat; enormes largitori omnium bonorum

Deo grates exsolvimus, qui vos de excelso prospexit, et in tanto virtutum culmine erexit. Quapropter, gloriose fili, quod ab apostolica sede per coepiscopum nostrum Mellitum postulastis, libenti animo concedimus: id est, ut vestra benignitas in monasterio in Dorovernensi civitate constituto, quod sanctus doctor vester Augustinus, beatae memoriae Gregorii discipulus, sancti Salvatoris nomini consecravit, cui ad praesens praeesse dignoscitur dilectissimus frater noster Laurentius, licenter per omnia monachorum regulariter viventium habitationem statuat: apostolica auctoritate decernentes, ut ipsi vestrae salutis praedicatores monachi, monachorum gregem sibi associent, et eorum vitam sanctam tum moribus exornent. Quae omnia decreta si quis successorum vestrorum regum, sive episcoporum, clericorum, sive laicorum irrita facere tentaverit, a principe apostolorum Petro, Petro, et a cunctis successoribus suis anathematis vinculo subjaceat, quoadusque quod temerario ausu peregit, Deo placita satisfactione poeniteat, et hujus inquietudinis veram emendationem faciat. In Christo valeas, domine fili.

The Scriptorium Project is the work of a small group of lay people of various apostolic churches who are interested in the preservation, transmission, and translation of the works of the early and medieval church. Our efforts are to make the works of the church fathers accessible to anyone who might have an interest in Christian antiquities and the theological, philosophical, and moral writings that have become the bedrock of Western Civilization.

To-date, our releases have pulled from the Greek, Syriac, Georgian, Latin, Celtic, Ethiopian, and Coptic traditions of Christianity, and have been pulled from sundry local traditions and languages.

Other Titles and Translations by D.P. Curtin:

First Book of Ethiopian Maccabees (2018)
Chronicon by Eutrandus of Ticino (2019)
Decrees of Aethelbert by St. Aethelbert, King of Kent (2019)
The Measure to be taxed for Penance by St. Columba of Iona (2019)
Protoevangelium of James: Greek and English Texts (2019)
Edicts of the Synod of Paris by Chlothar II, King of Franks (2019)
The Life of St. Desiderius by Sisebut, King of Visigoths (2019)
The Synod of Rome by St. Boniface IV of Rome (2019)
Letter to Pope Theodore by Victor of Carthage (2020)
The Decree of 610 by Gundemar, King of Visigoths (2020)
Laws of the Church by Chlothar III, King of Franks (2020)
Donations by St. Aethelbert, King of Kent (2020)
The Mystical Interpretation by St. Aileran the Wise (2020)
Laws of the Church by St. Dagobert II, King of Franks (2020)
The Old Nubian Miracle of St. Mena (2021)
About Fifteen Problems by St. Albertus Magnus (2022)
Testament of Some Former Things by John Scotus Eriugena (2022)
The Georgian Synaxarium (2022)
Instructions: Counsel for Novices by St. Ammonas the Hermit (2022)
The Syriac Menologium and Martyrology (2022)
Book on Religious Exercise and Quiet by St. Isaiah the Solitary (2022)
Vision of Theophilus by St. Cyril of Alexandria (2022)
On Fate (De Fato) by St. Albertus Magnus (2023)
Fragments of 'Chronicle' by Hippolytus of Thebes (2023)
Life of the Blessed Theotokos by Epiphanius Monachus (2023)
Syriac Life of John the Baptist by Serapion the Presbyter (2023)
Second Book of Ethiopian Maccabees (2023)